Contents

KT-226-278

'Higher, Faster, Further' is the motto of the Olympic Games, and field athletic events are all about throwing further or jumping higher or longer than the rest. Athletes pit themselves against the very best in their sport in rounds of competition. With each jump, vault or throw, they strain every sinew trying to gain precious centimetres which can be the difference between success and defeat.

Eight Events

There are eight main field athletics sports. They are divided into four throwing events: javelin, shot put, discus and hammer and four jumping events: long jump, high jump, triple jump and pole vault. Each event places great demands on the athletes' minds and bodies as, to succeed in competition, they must perfect every stage of their throw or jump. At a junior level, at school or in after school sports clubs, these events can be great fun to try out and see which most suit you and which you most enjoy. As you progress at one or more field events, there are likely to be local, schools and regional athletics meetings where you can compete against others.

A young athlete celebrates recording his best ever distance in the high jump. This is known as a personal best, or PB for short.

High jumpers need incredible spring and flexibility to leap up and over the bar and clear it with the whole of their body. The competition can be intense, as once a number of athletes clear a certain height, the bar is raised by a small number of centimetres.

Field Athletics

Clive Gifford

W
FRANKLIN WATTS
LONDON • SYDNEY

First published in 2008 by
Franklin Watts
338 Euston Road
London NW1 3BH

Franklin Watts Australia
Level 17/207 Kent Street
Sydney NSW 2000

Series editor: Jeremy Smith
Art director: Jonathan Hair

**Series designed and created for
Franklin Watts by Storeybooks.**
Designer: Rita Storey
Editor: Nicola Edwards
Photography: Tudor Photography,
    Banbury

A CIP catalogue record
for this book is available
from the British Library.

Dewey classification: 796.43
ISBN: 978 0 7496 8341 2
Printed in China

Franklin Watts is a division of
Hachette Children's Books, an Hachette Livre
UK company.
www.hachettelivre.co.uk

Note: At the time of going to press, the statistics
and player profiles in this book were up to date.
However, due to some players' active
participation in the sport, it is possible that some
of these may now be out of date.

Picture credits
Getty/Michael Steele /Allsport pp 7 and 25,
Michael Steele/Getty Images pp 21 and 27.

Every attempt has been made to clear copyright.
Should there be any inadvertent omission please
apply to the publisher for rectification.

Cover images: Tudor Photography, Banbury.

All photos posed by models.
Thanks to Hannah Bryan, Rashid Olubaji, Shana
Parker and Tasha Trigger.

The Publisher would like to thank Banbury
Harriers Athletic Club for their help.

Taking part in sport
is a fun way to get fit, but
like any form of physical
exercise it has an element of
risk, particularly if you are unfit,
overweight or suffer from any
medical conditions. It is
advisable to consult a healthcare
professional before beginning
any programme
of exercise.

The world's leading heptathlete, Carolina Kluft of Sweden, makes a shot put attempt at the 2006 European Athletics Championships. Heptathletes and decathletes have to be highly skilled in a range of field events as well as fast on the track.

Multi-Sport Events

There are two athletics competitions which combine a range of field events with running and hurdling events on the track. The male decathlon contains 10 events including long jump, shot put, high jump, discus, pole vault and javelin. The women's heptathlon is a seven event competition including high jump, shot put, long jump and javelin. These are considered the ultimate tests for an athlete.

Your Coach

For a junior athlete, listening to the advice of an experienced coach is essential to success. Good coaches can help prepare a suitable training plan for your age and ability. They can also offer on-the-spot guidance about your throwing or jumping technique. Little adjustments in technique can often yield big improvements in performance, so always pay full attention to what coaches show and tell you.

Ancient Origins

Some field athletics events have an incredibly long history. Javelin competitions, for instance, developed out of the spear throwing competitions which were held during the time of the Ancient Egyptians and possibly even longer ago. A number of field athletics events, including forms of long jump and discus, became part of the Ancient Olympics. These were games held by the Ancient Greeks every four years between 776 BCE and about 393 CE. The idea of the Ancient Greek games was revived in the 1890s to become the modern Olympics. By the 1900s all eight events were included for men. Field athletics events for women took longer to arrive with the last two, the pole vault and hammer throw, making their first Olympics appearance in 2000.

A Multi-talented Athlete

Eric Lemming (Sweden), former world record holder in the javelin, came fourth in the high jump, the pole vault and the hammer throw at the 1900 Olympics. He even entered the discus competition, coming eighth.

Equipment and Clothing

Field athletics events are held in an athletics stadium or sometimes in an open field. Some events, such as the high jump and long jump, are also performed inside indoor arenas. Most field athletics events, though, occur outdoors.

Runways and Circles

Each event in field athletics has its own marked out area. For the discus, hammer throw and shot put, this is a circle which, in the case of the discus and hammer, is usually surrounded by a safety cage. For the javelin, pole vault and the long and high jumps, the athletes begin at one end of a long strip of track-like area called a runway. This gives them the space to build up speed before attempting their throw, jump or vault.

▲ This athlete sprints down the long jump runway before making a jump.

Landing Zones

All throwing events have a marked out area, called the sector or landing zone, inside which the discus, shot or javelin must fall for the throw to be legal and be allowed. Officials are on hand to judge whether the implement has landed within the landing zone and whether the athlete stayed inside the correct area when completing the attempt.

Discus and hammer throws take place in a circle surrounded by a wire netting safety cage.
▼

Always push a javelin up into a ▶ vertical position.
▼

This girl is wearing typical clothing for field athletics including a vest in her athletics club colours over a cotton T-shirt

Lightweight stretchy shorts offer support.

As an athlete progresses, they may invest in specialised shoes for their event such as these shoes for discus (top) or long jumps (above).

Low-cut cotton socks soak up sweat.

Good quality training shoes should fit snugly and have cushioning inside.

Safety

Field athletics sports can be dangerous unless competitors and spectators follow all rules and guidelines. Never ever stray onto a runway or landing zone. Always carry any throwing implement in a safe way as shown to you by your coach. For example, always carry a heavy shot cradled securely in both hands and walk, never run, in a field athletics area.

Clothing

Clothing for young field athletes is straightforward – a vest or singlet and a pair of running shorts, and good quality trainers. Some young long jumpers use sprinting spikes instead of trainers. These are lightweight shoes with spikes on the front part of the sole to give grip on a track or runway. Top adult athletes have specialized clothing often made of a stretchy material which hugs the body and supports it. Some athletes choose to wear an all-in-one outfit. As female athletes grow older and their bodies develop, they may wear athletic support bras under their singlet or use a special sports top instead.

The Shot Put

The shot put takes place in a 2.135-metre wide circle. Competitors must not leave the circle until their shot has landed. The thrower enters the back of the circle, makes the shot putting attempt and then leaves via the back of the circle.

The Shot

The shot is a solid ball usually made of brass or iron. The shot comes in a range of different weights depending on the age of the thrower and whether they're a boy or girl (see panel). Many shot putters dip their hands in a tray of powdered chalk which helps them improve their grip.

▲ The shot put circle features a 10 centimetre wooden stopboard at the front which athletes can use to brace their front leg against. The landing sector is a 40 degree arc from the front of the circle.

SHOT WEIGHTS

	Age				
Gender	11-12	13-14	15-16	17-19	Adult
Male	3.25kg	4kg	5kg	6kg	7.26 kg
Female	2.72kg	3.25kg	4kg	4kg	4kg

The O'Brien Technique

1 The thrower enters the circle, stands at the back and focuses. She gets into position, leaning out of the back of the circle with the shot cradled in her neck and her non-throwing arm out for balance. Her back faces the front of the circle.

2 With her body coiled like a spring, the athlete stretches out her free leg as she pushes off her supporting leg.

Different Techniques

Beginners usually start with the most basic throw from a standing position. They crouch low and drive from a low to high position as their body and arm straighten to propel the shot put forwards. To gain extra distance, one of two more advanced techniques can be used. Using the rotational technique, throwers spin round on the balls of their feet in a similar way to the discus throw (see pages 14-15). The linear technique is named after the American shot putter Parry O'Brien, who developed it in the 1950s. He became the first man to record a throw of over 19 metres.

The shot is cradled in the hand, so that it doesn't touch the palm. It is held by the three middle fingers. The thumb and little finger are placed to the sides and a little towards the front to help steady and balance it.

4 The athlete's front leg is braced, meaning held firm. The back leg straightens quickly, providing much of the power in the action. The body unwinds to turn to face the front.

The back leg makes a low hop across the circle as the athlete starts to uncoil and turn her body. Her front leg drives towards the stopboard.

5 The arm extends quickly. It passes close by the neck and powers the shot away off the fingers upwards and forwards. The arm follows through in the direction of the flying shot. The athlete has to be careful to ensure she does not overbalance and step out of the circle. Many athletes switch feet after their follow-through and try to crouch down to avoid toppling forward.

The Javelin

The javelin throw depends on speed, timing and excellent body position as much as power. Good throws rely on the athlete releasing the javelin at the correct angle and with the javelin in line with the target. In a full javelin throw, athletes first build up speed along a long strip of track called a runway. Then, with accurate footwork and fast body and arm movements, they pull the javelin past their body before releasing it upwards and forwards.

The Javelin and Rules

The javelin is usually made from metal or fibreglass and has a rubberised or corded area near its middle called the grip where it is held. The javelin must be thrown over the shoulder, not slung underarm. Athletes often practise getting the basics of the throw right by using a standing throw before gradually

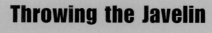

Throwing the Javelin

1 Having carefully measured out her run-up, the athlete begins at the far end of the runway. The athlete builds up her speed along the runway whilst carrying the javelin above shoulder height pointing towards the target. Her arm is slightly bent at the elbow.

2 In the space of two strides down the runway, the javelin is withdrawn. The athlete's throwing arm stretches backwards as her chest and shoulders turn to the side. The right knee drives up high to make the second-from-last step, called the crossover stride.

There are three ways to grip a javelin but this, the split-finger grip, is recommended for new throwers.

This thrower's foot has landed well over the scratch line. This will mean that her throw is invalid and won't count.

building up all the important footwork required. With a full throw, the athlete must be careful not to cross the line at the end of the runway called the scratch line. Once the javelin is released, its front tip, called the point, must touch the ground first for a throw to be legal.

3 *The athlete lands on her right foot with her body leaning back. Her free leg drives forward to make the last stride. At the same time, the rear leg bends to help push the hips forward and arch the body a little.*

4 *The athlete turns her chest and shoulders forwards. The right hip comes underneath the right shoulder. The throwing arm is whipped through with the elbow high and the javelin released as the arm goes past the head.*

5 *The rear leg continues to follow through after the javelin is released. The athlete bends this leg to stay balanced and to avoid overstepping the scratch line.*

The Discus

The discus is one of the oldest of all field event sports, first performed over 2,700 years ago. Throwers turn and release a flat, disc-shaped object, the discus, from inside a 2.5m wide throwing circle. Just like the javelin, the timing and the angle at which the discus is released are crucial in generating long throws.

This is the most common way to grip the discus. The discus is held loosely in the palm with the thumb on top to steady it and with the rim resting on the fingertips.

Brace and Release

A vital factor in a good discus throw is to have a firmly braced non-throwing side of the body as the throw is made. This acts as a support or platform for the rest of the body and throwing arm to move forward. Athletes release the discus as their chest faces forwards and their arm is extended and in line with their shoulders. The discus leaves the

Rotational Throw

1 The athlete stands facing the back of the circle with her knees flexed. After some preliminary swings to build momentum, the athlete begins to turn, shifting her body weight to the foot on the non-throwing side.

2 The athlete rotates on the ball of her foot, leading with her hips and with her shoulders following. Her head and upper body remain upright. Her non-throwing arm is out to help balance.

hand at an ideal angle of 30-40°, flying off the athlete's forefinger. This makes the discus spin clockwise, allowing it to slice through the air, stay stable and, as a result, travel further.

The Rotational Throw

Athletes learn the discus throwing technique by performing standing throws. But to obtain far greater distance, they need to perform a turn before they throw. This has an effect like winding up a spring: it builds speed and power. Good footwork, timing and balance are necessary for the one and a half turns in the circle to be performed well. It is very easy to lose control in the turn, become unbalanced and end up throwing the discus off line and at too steep or too shallow an angle. The key is to build up your turning speed in training and not to spin so fast that you lose control.

▲

When making preliminary swings before the main throw, your non-throwing hand can come up and underneath to support the discus at the top of each swing.

3 *The athlete turns to face the front of the circle for the second time. The non-throwing foot lands near the front of the circle. The movement of the legs guides the athlete's movement with the body following next. The throwing arm lags behind the rest of the movement but will whip through at the end.*

4 *With her shoulders facing the front, the athlete straightens her body. Her arm is whipped round and the discus released in an explosive movement. Her fingers press down the edge of the disc as it is released. This helps it spin away. After release, the athlete aims to regain her balance and to stay inside the circle.*

The Hammer

The hammer is a heavy ball and chain which is thrown inside a circle protected by a safety cage. The athlete winds up a big throw by swinging the hammer round and round, building up speed before timing the hammer's release. The hammer can be a daunting event to learn so coaches use many techniques and aids, including hammers on shortened chains and a ball inside a netting bag, in order to make it a little easier to get used to.

Equipment

The hammer for an adult thrower consists of a ball weighing 7.2kg for men and 4kg for women (weights for juniors tend to be less) attached to a sturdy steel wire between 96 and 98.5cm long. This is attached to a 11cm wide triangular handle gripped by the thrower who is allowed to wear protective gloves. The action takes place inside the hammer circle which is surrounded by a safety cage. This circle is the same size as the shot put circle, but has no stopboard.

Grip and Stance

The hammer handle is gripped first in the left hand if you're right-handed with the handle running along the base of the fingers. The right hand closes over the left.

Throwing the Hammer

1 Entering the circle, the thrower stands at the back of the circle ready to start her preliminary swings of the hammer.

2 The thrower swings the hammer up, back and round, usually for two complete turns during the preliminary swings. She aims to build up a good rhythm.

3 The thrower starts to turn, pivoting round on her left foot as she crosses the circle. She keeps her back straight and arms extended.

The thrower stands with feet relatively wide apart, with their back straight throughout the throw and with their knees flexed.

Swings and Turns

The first swings of the hammer are to build up some basic speed. Athletes pull the hammer across their body keeping their arms straight and shoulders level. During the preliminary swings, the hammer is swung so that it rises high behind you and falls when in front of you on these swings.

As the hammer swings anticlockwise, throwers start turning themselves around their left foot if right-handed and vice versa. They will make three or four complete turns with the hammer swinging smoothly round and from a low to high position on each turn. The speed of the hammer should be increasing with each turn. This takes great strength to counteract the force of the hammer swinging round and also excellent timing.

Delivery

The delivery phase begins as soon as the thrower's right foot makes contact with the ground at the end of the turns. As the hammer reaches its low point in its final swing, throwers straighten their legs sharply and with power.

Release

The hammer is released at the high point over the thrower's left shoulder so that it flies upwards and forwards. Ideally, it is released at an angle of approximately 45 degrees, with the thrower's hands rising high above the head.

The thrower continues to turn, building up speed, but all the time using her strength to control the swing of the hammer.

The thrower enters the delivery phase. The hammer is at the low point of its swing. As it rises, the thrower stands tall, driving her legs straight.

As the hammer rises, the thrower releases it over her shoulder. She lets go of the hammer handle and watches the hammer fly up and forwards.

17

The High Jump

High jumping is all about clearing a horizontal bar or crossbar without knocking it off from its supports known as uprights or standards. High jumpers make a springy run-up before driving their body up and over the bar.

High jumpers are allowed a number of attempts, normally three, at a set height. If they fail to clear the bar on all three attempts, then they are out of the competition. The remaining jumpers continue competing with the bar raised a set amount (usually 5cm but sometimes 3cm or 1cm) until only one jumper clears a set height and wins the competition. If two jumpers are tied at the same height, then the countback system is used where the number of failed attempts beforehand is taken into account.

The Fosbury Flop

The simplest form of high jump technique is called the scissors kick, but for greater heights and when a full crash mat is

The Fosbury Flop

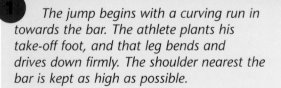

1 The jump begins with a curving run in towards the bar. The athlete plants his take-off foot, and that leg bends and drives down firmly. The shoulder nearest the bar is kept as high as possible.

2 Driving powerfully off his take off leg, he leaps almost straight upwards. Lift is increased by the knee of the other leg and the arms pumping upwards vigorously. His hips lift as he rises and his body turns.

positioned for the jumpers' safety, the Fosbury Flop is recommended. This technique is named after the 1968 Olympic high jump champion Dick Fosbury, who invented the technique a year earlier. This technique is a powerful yet controlled fling of the body and legs upwards and backwards over the bar.

To perform the scissors technique, this high jumper leaps up sideways to the bar and with a straight back, lifts his leading leg up and over the bar. His take-off leg follows up and over the bar in a scissors-like movement. In a good jump the athlete lands securely on both feet.

3 As the athlete rises, his head and then shoulders travel over the bar first. The jumper arches his back and tries to keep his body relaxed.

4 The athlete keeps his hips high. Once his hips clear the bar, he snaps his legs straight at the knee to lift them up and over, pulling in his heels to stop his feet clipping the bar.

The Pole Vault

The pole vault is arguably the most spectacular of all field events. A vaulter runs up and plants a flexible pole into a slot called the vaulting box. The pole bends and then straightens, carrying and catapulting the athlete up and over the bar.

Approach and Take-Off

The pole is held as high as possible as its other end is lowered and slid into the vaulting box. The speed of the vaulter's approach run will cause the bar to bend.

The pole vaulter holds the pole at one end with the other end lifted above the horizontal. Some vaulters hold the pole almost vertically. He begins his approach sprint keeping the pole balanced. The vaulter will lower the pole to a horizontal position as he gets to within a few strides of the bar.

Yelena Isinbayeva

Date of Birth: June 3rd, 1982

Nationality: Russian

Height: 1.74m

Isinbayeva trained as a gymnast until the age of 15 but was thought to be too tall to win the top competitions. She took up pole vaulting instead and began performing well in European and world junior events. In 2004, she won an Olympic gold medal. The following year she broke the women's pole vault record an astonishing nine times, becoming the first woman to clear five metres in competition.

Yelena Isinbayeva drives her legs upwards as her pole bends during a vault. In February 2008, she broke the women's indoor world record with a vault of 4.95m

Take Off and Flight

With the vaulter's hands high above the head, the front leg drives up high at the knee. The pole bends sharply then starts straightening, carrying the athlete high off the ground.

Clearing The Bar

The vaulter drives their feet and hips up towards the bar and performs a half turn. They arch their body, keeping their stomach tight, to clear the bar without knocking it off.

The pole used in a pole vault is usually between four and five metres long. It is made of highly flexible materials to allow it to bend yet carry a vaulter's weight. Your coach will select the correct pole for you.

Raising the Bar

Sergei Bubka broke the pole vault world record 35 times during his long career! He became the first athlete to vault six metres and set the current world record of 6.14 in 1994.

The vaulter's trailing leg has swung up and through so that the athlete is in an upside-down position. He stays as close to the pole as possible with his feet and hips directly above the head. This position is called the rock-back.

The athlete times the moment he lets go of the pole to avoid touching the bar. Getting his arms clear of the bar, he falls and aims to land on his back on the crash mat to absorb the impact of the fall.

The Long Jump

The long jump is the most natural of field athletics events but still needs large amounts of training. A long jumper builds up speed along the 45m long runway, then drives forward and upward at take-off before landing in the sandpit.

Sprinting Start

Speed is the key to long jump success but this has to be channelled into a controlled, sustained jump. Jumpers need to accelerate hard as they travel from a standing start along the runway. The more speed from their runway sprint that can be smoothly transferred into the jump, the longer the jump is likely to be.

A long jumper aims for the take-off foot to get as close as possible to the strip of clay at the front of the take-off board without touching it. Athletes work with their coach to work out what is the best length of run-up for them. An adult athlete may

The Long Jump

1 After measuring out her run-up carefully, the jumper begins her run-up. Her body leans forward as she sprints hard, pumping her arms to build speed.

2 After accelerating from a standing start along the runway, the jumper reaches top speed and uncurls from the forward lean so that she is running upright. The jumper aims for a smooth, even pattern of strides, keeping her body and hands relaxed and head upright as she focuses down the runway.

3 Reaching the take-off board, the jumper drives hard and powerfully off her take-off foot. She thinks of her leg striking down and back to propel them up and forward.

choose 24 paces whilst a younger athlete may choose 14. Leaving an object on the runway to mark the start of your run-up is only allowed in training and not in competition.

modelling clay

▲ The take-off board with a strip of modelling clay marking the scratch line. If any part of a jumper's foot crosses the scratch line and leaves a mark in the clay, the attempt will be a no-jump.

▲ Jumps are measured from the front edge of the take-off board to the closest mark made in the sand by a jumper. This is a vital reason why a jumper needs to fall forward on landing if possible.

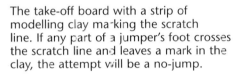

4 *The jumper swings her other leg up and through vigorously. There are different techniques performed once in the air. Here, the jumper performs the hang style with her feet up but the legs lagging behind the body at first. The jumper brings her legs and arms forward, avoiding the sand before landing.*

5 *On landing, the jumper lets her legs buckle, bending at the knees so that she telescopes down into the hole made by her feet. She throws her arms forwards and down. The aim is to land ahead of where the feet hit the sand. Sitting down or placing a hand back as they land can lose jumpers many precious centimetres of distance.*

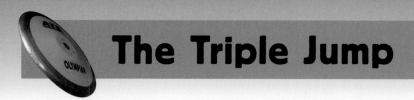

The Triple Jump

In a triple jump an athlete powers down the runway before performing a hop, then a step, and finally a jump into a sandpit. The athlete aims to make the three movements as smooth as possible.

Performed on the long jump runway and pit, the triple jump is the ultimate test of coordination and is usually only attempted after an athlete has some long jump experience. The jumper builds up speed along the runway in the approach phase before planting a foot to perform the first stage, the hop. The athlete hops forward landing on the same leg then performs a long step where they land on the other foot. The jump ends with a jump into the sand pit.

Profile: Jonathan Edwards

Date of Birth: May 10th, 1966

Nationality: British

Height: 1.83m

In 1995, Jonathan Edwards stunned the world of athletics with a series of staggeringly-long triple jumps first at the European Cup and then at the World Championship, where he broke the world record twice within 20 minutes. His longest jump of 18.29m still stands as a world record. Edwards won Olympic gold in 2000, six European Cup triple jump competitions and the 1995 and 2001 World Championships before retiring in 2003.

Jonathan Edwards performs a triple jump at the 2001 Norwich Union International athletics meeting in Glasgow, Scotland.

The Triple Jump

The jumper sprints hard down the runway with her head up and her arms pumping. Her speed may be a little lower than a long jump approach but she aims for a strong rhythm.

The athlete aims to hit the take-off board with her foot without crossing the scratch line. She performs the hop, pawing at the ground with her take-off foot and springing forward. She keeps her body upright and swings her arms.

The jumper drives her front leg upwards and forward and then brings her take-off leg through, extending her lower leg ahead of her body and then driving the leg downwards. She lands on her take-off foot to perform the step movement of the jump.

Pushing off strongly, the jumper leaps long and low with her leading leg swinging through to help pull her forward. The leg is raised at the knee so that the thigh is almost parallel with the ground.

As the foot of the leading leg makes contact with the ground, the leg is extended powerfully to perform the jump. Both arms swing through strongly. The jumper's take-off leg then has to travel forward quickly so that both feet are ahead of her. The jumper aims for as much time in the air as possible before landing.

25

In Competition

Top field athletes train exceptionally hard to win the chance to test themselves against the very best at a series of major competitions held all over the world.

Before every training session or competition, athletes must warm up and stretch their body's key muscles. This not only lessens the chance of injury, it also gives your body the best chance of performing well.

Training to Succeed

Field athletes work hard on their throwing or jumping technique, practising it regularly. They also aim to build not only their strength and speed but their flexibility – the range of movement part of the body can make. Drills are exercises which are repeated a number of times. Long jumpers, for example, might work on improving their sprinting speed by performing a series of short, explosive sprint drills. These can help condition their muscles to work at a faster rate.

Following the Rules

In competition, a field athlete's equipment is checked and each athlete is allowed a set number of attempts at their event. They must take each of their attempts in the order assigned to them. Officials watch the attempts carefully to judge if each jump or throw is valid. In big competitions, there is often a qualifying competition with the athletes who record the best jumps or throws going through to the final.

Major Competitions

Elite field athletes are professional (paid to play) sportspeople who attend many major competitions. An athlete and his or her coach will try to tailor their training and appearances so that they peak at one or several important competitions in the year. The biggest competition of all is the Summer Olympics. Held every four years, winning an Olympic gold medal is a highlight of any field athlete's career but qualification can be tough and rigorous.

Second only to the Olympics, the World Athletics Championships have been held since 1983 and now occur every two years. The championships are always held in a different year to the Olympics with the 2007 event held in Osaka, Japan and the 2009 competition in Berlin, Germany.

Golden League

The IAAF Golden League is a series of six athletics meetings. Any athlete who comes first in their event at all six meets gets the chance to win a share or all of a jackpot worth one million US dollars. In 2007 the jackpot was shared by a 400m runner and pole vaulter, Yelena Isinbayeva (see page 20). In previous years, triple jumpers

Christian Olsson and Tatyana Lebedeva have both triumphed.

European Cup and Commonwealth Games

First held in 1930 as a competition for territories of the British Empire, the Commonwealth Games now attracts athletes from over 70 nations and is held once every four years. The 2010 games will be held in Delhi in India. Another important competition, the European Cup, began in the 1960s. National athletics teams compete in different leagues, with the superleague containing eight teams.

Jan Zelezny gets into position to launch a throw during the 2006 European Championships held in Sweden. Zelezny remains the Olympic, World Championships and World record holder in men's javelin.

Jan Zelezny

Date of Birth: June 16th, 1966

Nationality: Czech

Height: 1.86m

The greatest male javelin thrower of all time, Zelezny has won three Olympic gold medals (1992, 1996 and 2000) and one silver (1988) as well as three World Championships. No other athlete has come within five metres of his world record throw of 98.48m, whilst he has thrown over 90m more than 50 times.

Statistics and Records

World Records (Men)

High Jump	2.45m	Javier Sotomayor (Cuba)	1993 Salamanca
Pole Vault	6.14m	Sergey Bubka (Ukraine)	1994 Sestriere
Long Jump	8.95m	Mike Powell (USA)	1991 Tokyo
Triple Jump	18.29m	Jonathan Edwards (UK)	1995 Gothenburg
Shot Put	23.12m	Randy Barnes (USA)	1990 Los Angeles
Discus	74.08m	Jürgen Schult (Germany)	1986 Neubrandenburg
Hammer	86.74m	Yuriy Sedykh (Russia)	1986 Stuttgart
Javelin	98.48m	Jan Zelezny (Finland)	1996 Jena

World Records (Women)

High Jump	2.09m	Stefka Kostadinova (Bulgaria)	1987 Rome
Pole Vault	5.01m	Yelena Isinbayeva (Russia)	2005 Helsinki
Long Jump	7.52m	Galina Chistyakova (Russia)	1988 St.Petersburg
Triple Jump	15.50m	Inessa Kravets (Ukraine)	1995 Gothenburg
Shot	22.63m	Natalya Lisovskaya (Russia)	1987 Moscow
Discus	76.80m	Gabriele Reinsch (Germany)	1988 Neubrandenburg
Hammer	77.41m	Tatyana Lysenko (Russia)	2006 Zhukovskiy
Javelin	71.70m	Osleidys Menéndez (Cuba)	2005 Helsinki

Most Dominance in the European Cup

Russia Women's team with 11 wins in a row (1997-2007)

First Four-time Winner of an Olympic Field Athletics Event

Al Oerter (USA) in the discus (1956, 1960, 1964 and 1968).

Most World Records Broken During a Career

Sergei Bubka (Ukraine) with 35 world records in the pole vault.

Cuban high jumper, Javier Sotomayor has cleared the height of 2.30 metres or higher at a staggering 227 athletics meetings.

Bob Beamon (USA) smashed the world record for the men's long jump with a huge leap of 8.90m at the 1968 Olympics. Although surpassed as the world record, it remains one of the longest standing of all Olympic records.

Glossary and Websites

Acceleration An increase in an athlete's speed.

Approach The run-up made by an athlete before performing a jump or vault.

Countback A system used to work out the winner when two high jumpers or pole vaulters are tied at the same height.

Double arm shift When both arms are swung together in the triple or long jump.

Elite Top, usually professional, athletes.

Fosbury Flop A style of high jumping where the athlete travels over the bar head first and face up.

Leading leg The first leg to leave the ground in a jump.

Personal Best Sometimes shortened to PB, in field athletics this is an athlete's best ever distance or height for an event.

Scissors jump A style of high jump in which the legs make a scissors movement as they cross the bar.

Scratch line The line which, if crossed in throwing or jumping events, results in a foul jump or throw.

Stance An athlete's starting position.

Stopboard The wooden board at the front of a shot put circle against which an athlete can brace his or her foot.

Websites

www.ukathletics.net
The website of the governing body for the sport of athletics in the UK, packed with news, features and details of schemes and local clubs.

www.iaaf.org/statistics/records/index.html
Check out the world's latest records and personal bests at the website of the International Association of Athletics Federations (IAAF), the organization that runs world athletics.

www.olympic.org
Read profiles on famous field athletes and much more at the official website of the International Olympic Committee.

www.gbrathletics.com/sites.htm
An athletics statistics website with a terrific collection of links to other sites.

www.usatf.org
The home page of the United States Track and Field which governs athletics in America.

www.athletics.org.au
Athletics Australia's website is packed with athlete biographies, news and features and a section aimed at secondary school students.

Note to parents and teachers: every effort has been made by the Publishers to ensure that these websites are suitable for children, that they are of the highest educational value, and that they contain no inappropriate or offensive material. However, because of the nature of the Internet, it is impossible to guarantee that the contents of these sites will not be altered. We strongly advise that Internet access is supervised by a responsible adult.

Index